How We Use

Wood

Chris Oxlade

www.raintreepublishers.co.uk
Visit our website to find out more information about **Raintree** books.

To order:
 Phone 44 (0) 1865 888112
📠 Send a fax to 44 (0) 1865 314091
💻 Visit the Raintree bookshop at **www.raintreepublishers.co.uk** to browse our catalogue and order online.

First published in Great Britain by Raintree,
Halley Court, Jordan Hill, Oxford OX2 8EJ,
part of Harcourt Education.
Raintree is a registered trademark of
Harcourt Education Ltd.

Editorial: Nick Hunter
Design: Kim Saar
Picture Research: Heather Sabel and Amor
  Montes de Oca
Production: Alex Lazarus

Originated by Ambassador Litho Ltd.
Printed and bound in China by South China
Printing Company

ISBN 1 844 43262 9
08 07 06 05 04
10 9 8 7 6 5 4 3 2 1

British Library Cataloguing in Publication Data
Oxlade, Chris
How We Use Wood. - (Using Materials)
620.1'2
A full catalogue record for this book is available from
the British Library.

Acknowledgements
The publishers would like to thank the following
for permission to reproduce photographs:
Art Directors & TRIP (Helene Rogers) p. **13**; Corbis pp.
5 (Owaki – Kulla), **7** (Charles O'Rear), **11** (Zandria
Muench Beraldo), **14** (M. Angelo), **15** (Michael Boys),
20 (Dave G. Houser), **21** (Hans Georg Roth), **24**
(Robert Estall), **26**, **29**; Dwight Kuhn p. **18**; Harcourt
Education pp. **10**, **28** (Greg Williams); Jonah
Calinawan p. **16**; Mark Gibson p. **17**; Peter Kubal p. **8**;
Rick Wetherbee p. **9**; Visuals Unlimited pp. **4** (Dr
Richard Kessel & Dr C. Shih), **6** (Inga Spence), **12**
(David Wrobel), **19** (Michele Burgess), **22** (Joe
McDonald), **27** (Jeff Greenberg); Yves Tzaud p. **25**.

Cover photographs reproduced with permission
of Corbis.

Contents

Any words appearing in bold, **like this**, are explained in the Glossary.

Wood and its properties

All the things we use at home, school and work are made from materials. Wood is a material. We use wood for all sorts of different jobs. You can see wood being used wherever you go. For example, in the kitchen you might see wooden spoons. On a building site you could see whole houses made from wood.

This is what wood looks like through a microscope. You can see the long fibres that make up the wood.

Here, wood has been used to make chairs, walls and floors.

Properties tell us what a material is like. Most wood is strong. Some wood is light and some is heavy. Some wood is soft and some is hard. Wood comes in different colours and with different patterns. All wood is made up of long **fibres**. These make up the lines in wood.

Don't use it!

*The different properties of materials make them useful for different jobs. For example, wood **rots** if it gets damp. So we would not make an underground pipe from wood. It would soon rot and leak.*

Where does wood come from?

Wood is a **natural** material. It comes from trees. The trunk and branches of a tree are made of wood. The leaves are not. There are thousands of different sorts of trees. Each sort of tree gives us wood with different **properties**. For example, the wood from a pine tree is light in colour and quite soft, but the wood from an oak tree is darker and harder.

This tree was grown so people can use its wood. A new tree will be planted in its place.

The forestry industry

Huge areas of land are used to grow trees for wood. This is called the forestry **industry**. Trees take between 20 and 50 years to grow big enough to be used for wood. Then they are cut down and the branches are cut off. The trunks are carried to a sawmill. Here they are cut into long pieces and sold.

Planks cut from trees have to dry out before they are used.

Wood for fuel

A **fuel** is a material that we burn to make heat for cooking and keeping warm. Wood is a good fuel. That means it burns well. Wood only catches fire quickly when it is dry. Wet wood is hard to light. Logs for fires are made by cutting up tree trunks and thick branches. They need to be dried so they will burn well.

We use thin strips of wood called kindling to get a fire started because they catch light quickly.

This stove is designed to burn wood instead of other fuels.

Finding wood

In remote places fuels like gas, oil and coal are difficult to get or too expensive to buy. Here people use wood for cooking, heating and for making light. Sometimes their homes are surrounded by forests, so wood is easy to find. Sometimes all the wood has been used up and people have to walk many kilometres searching for twigs and branches.

Charcoal

If wood is burned with only a little air it smoulders slowly. Instead of turning to ash it turns into a black solid called charcoal. Artists use charcoal for drawing. Charcoal is a good fuel for barbecues because it burns slowly.

Wood for building

Wood is quite a strong material. Thin pieces of wood bend easily but thick pieces of wood are hard to bend. We use long, strong pieces of wood to make frames inside buildings. For example, wooden frames called trusses hold up roofs in houses. In some houses the walls are held up by a wooden frame, too.

These wooden frames will have houses built around them.

In some places in the world wood is used to build homes from tree trunks and branches.

Builders also use strong pieces of wood to hold up floors and for floorboards. Some houses have walls covered in wood called cladding. It keeps the wind and rain out of the house. Wooden cladding also looks good because wood is a **natural** material.

Don't use it!

Wood is strong enough for building houses, but not for building huge structures such as skyscrapers and long bridges. Materials like concrete and steel are much stronger.

Wooden furniture

The **properties** of wood mean that it is good for making furniture. Wood is strong and easy to cut and join. People also like its **natural** appearance. We make chairs, tables, beds, cupboards and shelves from wood. Soft furniture, such as sofas, have wooden frames hidden inside. We also use wood for doors.

All the parts of this chest of drawers are made from wood.

The join at the edge of this drawer is called a dovetail joint.

Furniture is made from many different sorts of wood. For example, pine makes light, cheap furniture. Mahogany makes beautiful dark furniture, but it is expensive because it is rare and takes a long time to grow.

Don't use it!
Wood must be dried properly before it is made into furniture. Furniture made from damp wood can twist and bend as the wood dries out quickly in a warm house. This is called warping.

Working with wood

Wood is easy to cut and shape with metal tools such as saws and chisels. Pieces are joined together with screws, nails, bolts or glue. The wooden parts of most pieces of furniture are cut out and shaped by machines.

Wood for decoration

Wood comes in different colours. Some woods are almost white. Some are yellowy, but most are brown. A few sorts are red. When a tree trunk or a branch is cut lengthways you see an interesting pattern of long wavy stripes. This pattern is called **grain**. Dark circles in the grain are called knots. The colour and pattern in the grain of wood makes it good for decoration.

Wood with beautiful swirls is called burlwood.

The patterns on this chair are made from skillfully cut pieces of veneer.

Dirt and water spoil wood. We can protect wood with **chemicals** such as oil and wax. They also help to make the grain show up clearly. Wood is not very hard. Painting wood with **varnish** helps to stop it getting scratched by harder materials such as metal.

Veneers

A **veneer** is a very thin sheet of wood. We use veneers with beautiful colour and grain to cover cheap wood or board. Craftspeople make patterns and pictures on furniture using small pieces of veneer made from different woods.

Wood for boards

A board is a wide, flat, thin piece of wood. We can cut only narrow boards, such as floorboards, from tree trunks because the trunks are narrow. Floorboards are strong and light and cheaper than metal or concrete.

Other types of wooden board are made by glueing smaller bits of wood together. Plywood is made by glueing thin strips of wood together in layers. The wood is laid so that the **grain** in one layer is at right angles to the grain in the layers above and below. This makes plywood very strong. We use plywood to make doors and floors.

This is the edge of a piece of plywood. You can see the edge of some layers and the ends of others.

This chipboard is being used as part of a frame for a house.

Boards from bits

Chipboard and fibreboard come from waste wood from a sawmill. Chipboard is made from small pieces of wood called chips. They are mixed with glue and the mixture is pressed flat until the glue dries. We use chipboard for making cupboards and worktops. Chipboard can be covered in **veneer** to make it look like real wood.

Wood for paper

The paper in this book is made from wood. So is newspaper, writing paper, paper for envelopes, card and cardboard. Paper is made from wood **fibres**, which are pressed together into a very thin sheet. Wood is used to make paper because the fibres are cheap and plentiful.

This is the edge of ripped paper seen through a microscope. You can see the ends of the wood fibres.

Wood pulp
has been put on to a wire mesh
to make this paper by hand.

Wood to paper

One out of every ten trees that are cut down is used to make paper. The wood is broken into tiny pieces and mixed with **chemicals** that separate the fibres from each other. This makes a thick fibre soup called wood pulp. The pulp is spread out, rolled flat and then dried to make the finished paper.

Wood afloat

Wood floats on water. This is because a piece of wood weighs less than the same amount of water. Very light wood, such as balsa wood, only sinks into the water a tiny bit. Heavy wood, such as teak, sinks in much further before it floats. The simplest boats are rafts made by tying logs or planks together.

This special raft in Fiji has been made from long, thin logs.

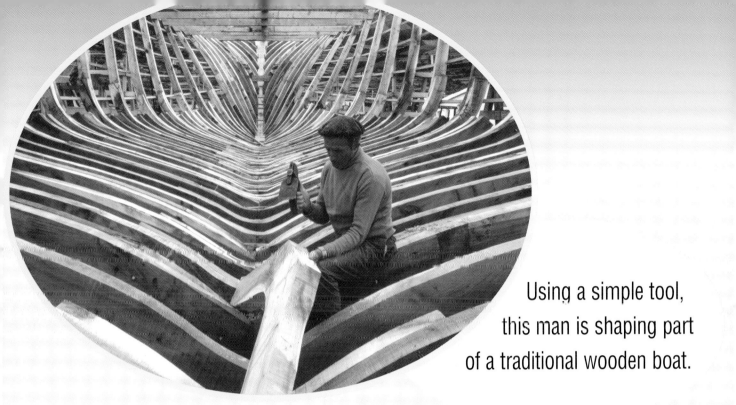

Using a simple tool, this man is shaping part of a traditional wooden boat.

Boat building

Small boats are made from wood because wood is easy to cut, shape and join with simple tools. The pieces of wood are joined tightly together to stop water leaking through the gaps between them. If the wood does get damp, it gets bigger and fills the gaps. Wooden boats must be painted or varnished to make them **waterproof** and stop the wood **rotting**.

Don't use it!

Shipbuilders do not use wood to build large ships such as oil tankers. They use metal instead. Metal is much stronger and can be made into huge pieces. Pieces of metal can also be joined more strongly than pieces of wood.

Preserving wood

When wood gets wet it **rots** away. It goes soft or crumbly and falls apart. Rotting is a **natural** process. It happens because tiny **organisms** grow on the wood. They break apart the wood's **fibres** and feed on them. If we use bare wood outdoors it rots away quickly. Wood in the ground, such as fence posts, rots very quickly because it is always wet. Animals, such as termites, also eat wood, making it weak.

A rotted wooden roof. The roof will have to be rebuilt.

Treating wood

We make sure that wood does not rot by using **chemicals** called **preservatives**. Organisms cannot grow on the wood because the preservative is poisonous to them. We can paint preservative on, or dip whole pieces of wood in a bath of preservative. We can also stop rot by painting or **varnishing** the surface of wood.

Woodworm

Old floorboards and pieces of furniture often have tiny holes in them. This is called woodworm. The holes are bored in the wood by young beetles called larvae. They eat the wood as they bore through it. Woodworm makes wood weak.

The preservative on this brush will soak into the wood, protecting it from rot.

Weaving wood

Small branches and thin strips of wood are **flexible**. They bend without snapping. This **property** makes them good for **weaving**. Weaving is done by passing the branches or strips of wood over and under each other. Panels for fences are made by weaving. Some panels are woven from wide, thin strips of wood. Others are woven from tree branches with their twigs and leaves stripped off.

This man is weaving a fence in a garden from bendy branches.

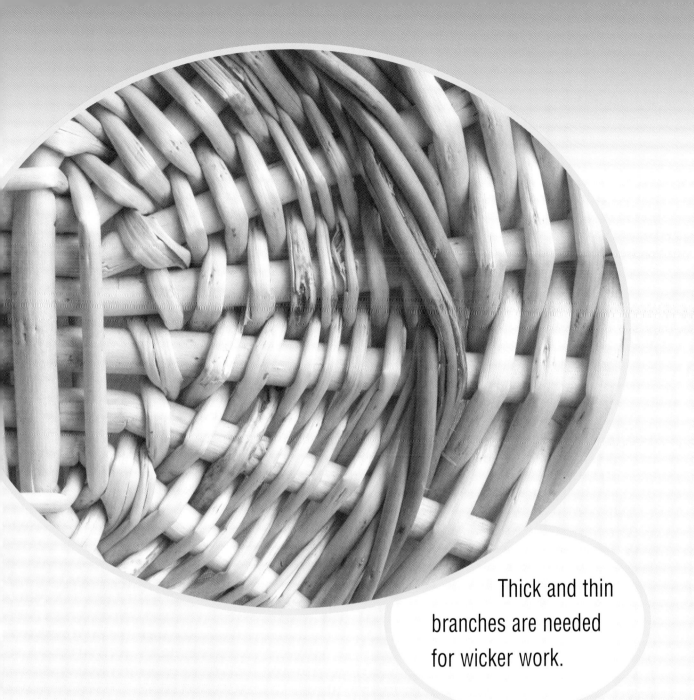

Thick and thin branches are needed for wicker work.

Wicker

We also weave wood to make chairs and baskets. Wicker is made by weaving thin branches from willow trees. Chairs made from wicker are light and strong. They also bend slightly, which makes them comfortable to sit on.

Wood for objects

Wood is a good material for making all sorts of everyday objects. You can find wooden objects in the kitchen such as mixing spoons. Your home might be decorated with pictures in wooden frames. All these things could be made with plastic instead, but people often prefer wood because it looks **natural**. Some wooden things, such as lollipop sticks, are very cheap to make so we can throw them away after using them.

Bottle corks are made from the thick bark of cork trees.

This horse's head has been carved from a big block of wood.

Wood carving

Wooden ornaments are made by carving wood. A **sculptor** starts with a block of wood. He or she cuts away pieces of the block with a chisel and hammer, leaving behind the wood that makes the shape. Wooden furniture is often decorated by carving, too.

Don't use it!

We do not make very tiny or complicated shapes from wood. They are too difficult to carve. Tiny and complicated parts for machines are made from plastic or metal instead. Wooden parts would wear out too quickly.

Wood and the environment

Wood is a **natural** material. We should never run out of wood because we can always grow more. However, some types of tree are running out because people have cut them down and not planted new ones. Many trees in the world's **rainforests** are being cut down for their valuable wood, like teak and mahogany. Some of these trees have taken more than a hundred years to grow and we can never replace them. Animals that live in the forest are also losing their homes.

Put newspapers, magazines and card into recycling bins.

These trees were specially grown for their wood.

Making paper from wood uses up lots of energy. It also uses **chemicals** that are dangerous to throw away. We can save energy and chemicals by using paper again. This is called **recycling**.

Don't use it!

We should not use wood without knowing where it comes from. We should only use wood that comes from forests that are specially grown for their wood. These are called **sustainable** *forests.*

Find out for yourself

The best way to find out more about wood is to investigate for yourself. Look around your home for wood, and keep an eye out for where wood is used through your day. Think about why wood was used for each job. What **properties** make it suitable? You will find the answers to many of your questions in this book. You can also look in other books and on the Internet.

Books to read

Science Answers: Grouping Materials, Carol Ballard (Heinemann Library, 2003)

Discovering Science: Matter, Rebecca Hunter (Raintree, 2003)

Science Files: Wood, Steve Parker (Heinemann Library, 2002)

Using the Internet

Try searching the Internet to find out about things to do with wood. Websites can change, so if one of the links below no longer works, don't worry. Use a search engine, such as www.yahooligans.com or www.internet4kids.com.
For example, you could try searching using the keywords 'forestry', 'boat building' and '**sustainable**'.

Websites

A great site, which explains all about different materials:
http://www.bbc.co.uk/schools/revisewise/science/materials/

A fun site that explains how wood is grown and used:
www.forestry.gov.uk

Glossary

chemical substance that we use to make other substances, or for jobs such as cleaning

fibre long, thin, bendy piece of material

flexible describes a material that can bend without snapping

fuel material that burns well, giving out lots of heat. Wood is a good fuel.

grain pattern of lines in wood. Grain is made by the wood's fibres.

industry group of organizations that do the same job. For example, iron making is an industry. So is coal mining.

natural describes anything that is not made by people

organism living thing

preservative chemical that helps to stop wood rotting

property quality of a material that tells us what it is like. Hard, soft, bendy and strong are all properties.

rainforest thick forest that grows where the weather is always wet and warm

recycle to use material from old objects to make new objects

rot process that makes wood weak and crumbly. It happens when tiny organisms eat away the wood.

sculptor person who designs and makes figures out of wood or other materials

sustainable source of material that never runs out. Sustainable forests are grown to supply wood.

varnish liquid that is painted on wood to protect the wood. Varnish goes hard when it dries.

veneer very thin sheet of wood

waterproof describes a material that does not let water pass through it

weave to make fabric by threading fibres or yarns under and over each other

Index

Titles in the *Using Materials* series include:

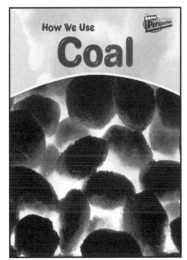

Hardback   1 844 43260 2

Hardback   1 844 43267 X

Hardback   1 844 43265 3

Hardback   1 844 43263 7

Hardback   1 844 43266 1

Hardback   1 844 43261 0

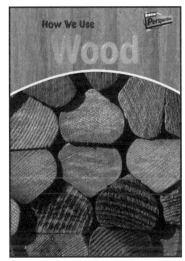

Hardback   1 844 43262 9

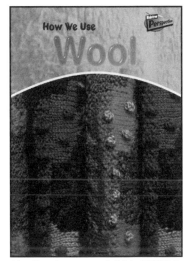

Hardback   1 844 43268 8

Find out about the other titles in this series on our website www.raintreepublishers.co.uk